DOG FOOD COOKBOOK FOR WEIGHT MANAGEMENT

Dr. Wesley Glasgow

DOG FOOD COOKBOOK FOR WEIGHT MANAGEMENT

DISCLAIMER

The content within this book reflects my thoughts, experiences, and beliefs. It is meant for informational and entertainment purposes. While I have taken great care to provide accurate information, I cannot guarantee the absolute correctness or applicability of the content to every individual or situation. Please consult with relevant professionals for advice specific to your needs.

TABLE OF CONTENTS

INTRODUCTION

Growing up, my passion for dogs was evident from an early age. As a child, I was fortunate enough to have loving parents who understood my deep connection with animals. When they surprised me with my first dog, Dan, I felt like the luckiest kid in the world. Dan wasn't just a pet; he was my loyal companion, my confidant, and my best friend.

I poured my heart and soul into caring for Dan. From long walks in the park to cozy cuddle sessions on the couch, we shared countless memories together. But perhaps the most significant expression of my love for Dan was through his meals. I showered him with treats, indulged him with table scraps, and even snuck him extra portions of his favorite foods. In my eyes, giving Dan everything he wanted to eat was an act of love.

However, as the years went by, I began to notice alarming changes in Dan's health. He became lethargic, struggled to move around, and gained an excessive amount of weight. Concerned for his well-being, I took Dan to the veterinarian, hoping for answers.

The diagnosis hit me like a ton of bricks: Dan had developed diabetes due to his obesity and poor diet. It was a wake-up call like no other. The veterinarian explained to me the critical role that nutrition plays in a dog's overall health and well-being. With a heavy heart, I realized that my well-intentioned gestures of love had inadvertently harmed my beloved companion.

Dan's meals underwent a complete transformation under the guidance of the veterinarian. He was put on a strict diet tailored to manage his diabetes and promote weight loss. Witnessing the transformative power of proper nutrition firsthand, I was inspired to delve deeper into the world of canine nutrition.

Fast forward twenty-five years, and I stand before you as Dr. Wesley Glasgow, a veterinarian and culinary enthusiast dedicated to improving the lives of dogs through the power of nutrition. My journey from a dog-loving child to a seasoned professional has been shaped by Dan's experience and the lessons I've learned along the way.

In my pursuit of knowledge, I have become a fervent advocate for healthy eating habits for dogs. Through my years of research, experimentation, and hands-on experience, I have uncovered the secrets to crafting nutritious and delicious meals that support optimal health and vitality in our four-legged friends.

Now, I invite you to join me on a journey of discovery—a journey that will transform the way you nourish and care for your canine companions. In this cookbook, I will share with you a collection of carefully curated recipes designed to promote weight management, boost energy levels, and enhance overall well-being in dogs.

But before we embark on this culinary adventure, let us pause to reflect on some essential questions:

- **How does the food we feed our dogs impact their health and longevity?**

- **What are the dangers and consequences of unhealthy eating habits for dogs?**

- **What are the advantages and benefits of adopting a nutritious and balanced diet for our furry friends?**

- **How can this cookbook empower you to take control of your dog's health and happiness?**

Through the pages that follow, we will explore these questions and more, uncovering the profound impact that proper nutrition can have on the lives of our beloved canine companions. Together, let us embark on a journey of discovery, enlightenment, and culinary delight—a journey that will nourish both body and soul.

Welcome to the Dog Food Cookbook for Weight Management—where every meal is a testament to the boundless love we share with our furry friends.

CHAPTER 1
Basics of Dog Nutrition

Proper nutrition is crucial for the overall health and well-being of your canine companion. Understanding the basics of dog nutrition ensures that you can provide your furry friend with the essential nutrients they need to thrive.

Essential Nutrients for Dogs

Dogs require a balanced diet consisting of various essential nutrients to maintain optimal health. These nutrients include:

1. **Proteins**: Essential for muscle growth, repair, and overall body function. High-quality animal-based proteins, such as chicken, beef, and fish, are ideal for dogs.

2. **Carbohydrates**: Serve as a source of energy for dogs. Whole grains like brown rice, oats, and barley are excellent sources of carbohydrates.

3. **Fats**: Provide energy, support cell function, and aid in nutrient absorption. Omega-3 and Omega-6 fatty acids, found in sources like fish oil and flaxseed, are beneficial for skin and coat health.

4. **Vitamins**: Play crucial roles in various bodily functions, including metabolism, immunity, and vision. Dogs require vitamins A, D, E, and B-complex vitamins, which can be obtained from a balanced diet.

5. **Minerals**: Important for bone health, nerve function, and enzyme activity. Calcium, phosphorus, potassium, and zinc are essential minerals for dogs.

6. **Water**: Vital for hydration, temperature regulation, and digestion. Always ensure your dog has access to clean, fresh water.

Recommended Daily Caloric Intake

The recommended daily caloric intake for dogs depends on various factors, including age, size, activity level, and overall health. Generally, adult dogs require between 25 to 30 calories per pound of body weight per day, while puppies and highly active dogs may need more.

To determine the specific caloric needs of your dog, consult with your veterinarian, who can provide personalized recommendations based on your dog's individual requirements.

Understanding Dog Food Labels

Understanding dog food labels is essential for selecting a high-quality diet for your canine companion. Here are key elements to look for:

1. **Ingredients List**: Ingredients are listed in descending order by weight. Look for whole food ingredients such as meat, vegetables, and grains. Avoid foods with excessive fillers, by-products, or artificial additives.

2. **Guaranteed Analysis**: Indicates the minimum percentages of crude protein, fat, fiber, and moisture in the food. Ensure these values meet your dog's nutritional needs.

3. **AAFCO Statement**: The Association of American Feed Control Officials (AAFCO) establishes nutritional standards for pet foods. Look for a statement indicating that the food is "complete and balanced" for your dog's life stage (e.g., adult maintenance, growth, or all life stages).

4. **Feeding Instructions**: Provide guidelines on how much to feed based on your dog's weight and life stage. Adjust portions as needed to maintain an ideal body condition.

CHAPTER 2
Creating a Healthy Meal Plan

A healthy meal plan is essential for maintaining your dog's overall well-being and managing their weight effectively. By designing balanced meals, controlling portions, and incorporating fresh ingredients, you can ensure your canine companion receives the nutrition they need to thrive.

Designing Balanced Meals for Weight Management

When creating a meal plan for your dog's weight management, focus on providing a balance of nutrients while controlling calorie intake. Here are some tips:

1. **Lean Proteins**: Include lean sources of protein such as chicken, turkey, lean beef, or fish. Protein helps maintain muscle mass while promoting satiety.

2. **Healthy Carbohydrates**: opt for complex carbohydrates like brown rice, sweet potatoes, and oats. These provide sustained energy and fibber for digestive health.

3. **Healthy Fats**: Incorporate sources of healthy fats such as salmon oil, flaxseed oil, or coconut oil. These fats support skin and coat health and provide essential fatty acids.

4. **Fruits and Vegetables**: Add a variety of fruits and vegetables to provide vitamins, minerals, and antioxidants. Examples include carrots, peas, blueberries, and apples.

5. **Portion Control**: Measure your dog's food portions according to their weight and energy needs. Avoid overfeeding, as excess calories can contribute to weight gain.

6. **Feeding Schedule**: Establish a consistent feeding schedule with set meal times. This helps regulate your dog's metabolism and prevents overeating.

Portion Control and Feeding Frequency

Portion control is crucial for managing your dog's weight and preventing obesity-related health issues. Follow these guidelines for portion control:

1. **Calculate Caloric Needs**: Determine your dog's daily caloric requirements based on factors such as age, weight, activity level, and body condition.

2. **Divide Meals**: Divide your dog's daily food allowance into multiple smaller meals throughout the day. This helps prevent overeating and keeps your dog satisfied.

3. **Use Measuring Tools**: Use a measuring cup or scale to accurately portion out your dog's meals. Avoid free-feeding, as it can lead to overconsumption.

4. **Monitor Body Condition**: Regularly assess your dog's body condition score to ensure they are maintaining a healthy weight. Adjust portion sizes as needed to achieve and maintain an ideal body condition.

Incorporating Fresh Ingredients

Incorporating fresh ingredients into your dog's meals provides essential nutrients and adds variety to their diet. Here are some ways to include fresh ingredients:

1. **Raw or Steamed Vegetables**: Offer a variety of fresh vegetables such as broccoli, spinach, and zucchini. These can be served raw or lightly steamed for easier digestion.

2. **Fresh Fruits**: Provide fresh fruits like bananas, strawberries, and watermelon as healthy, natural treats. Remove seeds and pits, and offer in moderation due to their natural sugar content.

3. **Herbs and Greens**: Add fresh herbs like parsley, basil, or mint to your dog's meals for added flavour and nutritional benefits.

4. **Supplements**: Consider adding fresh supplements like probiotics, digestive enzymes, or omega-3 fatty acids to support your dog's overall health and well-being.

OTHER BOOKS BY THE AUTHOR

DOG FOOD COOKBOOK FOR SENIOR DOGS

DOG FOOD COOKBOOK FOR PICKY EATERS

AIR FRYER DOG FOOD COOKBOOK

SLOW COOKER DOG FOOD COOKBOOK

DOG FOOD COOKBOOK FOR SENSITIVE STOMACH

SCAN THE QR CODE TO SEE MORE BOOKS BY AUTHOR

CHAPTER 3
Breakfast Ideas

Turkey and Vegetable Scramble

Cooking Time: 15 minutes

Servings: 2

Ingredients:

- 1 cup cooked turkey, diced
- 1/2 cup mixed vegetables (e.g., carrots, peas, broccoli), finely chopped
- 4 eggs
- 1 tablespoon olive oil

Instructions:

1. Heat olive oil in a skillet over medium heat.
2. Add mixed vegetables and cook until softened, about 5 minutes.
3. Add diced turkey to the skillet and cook for an additional 2-3 minutes.
4. In a bowl, whisk the eggs.
5. Pour the whisked eggs into the skillet with the turkey and vegetables.
6. Cook, stirring occasionally, until the eggs are fully cooked and scrambled, about 5-7 minutes.
7. Remove from heat and let cool before serving to your dog.

Nutritional Information: Protein: 18g, Fat: 12g, Carbohydrates: 3g, Calories: 190

Salmon and Sweet Potato Hash

Cooking Time: 20 minutes

Servings: 2

Ingredients:

- 1 cup cooked salmon, flaked
- 1/2 cup cooked sweet potato, diced
- 2 eggs
- 1 tablespoon coconut oil

Instructions:

1. Heat coconut oil in a skillet over medium heat.
2. Add diced sweet potato to the skillet and cook until lightly browned, about 5 minutes.
3. Add flaked salmon to the skillet and cook for an additional 2-3 minutes.
4. In a separate pan, fry the eggs to your desired doneness.
5. Divide the salmon and sweet potato mixture onto two plates.
6. Top each serving with a fried egg.
7. Let cool before serving to your dog.

Nutritional Information: Protein: 20g, Fat: 15g, Carbohydrates: 10g, Calories: 250

Chicken and Quinoa Breakfast Bowl

Cooking Time: 25 minutes

Servings: 2

Ingredients:

- 1 cup cooked chicken breast, shredded

- 1/2 cup cooked quinoa

- 1/4 cup cooked spinach, chopped

- 2 tablespoons plain Greek yogurt

Instructions:

1. In a bowl, combine shredded chicken, cooked quinoa, and chopped spinach.

2. Mix well until evenly combined.

3. Divide the mixture into two bowls.

4. Top each bowl with a tablespoon of plain Greek yogurt.

5. Serve to your dog at room temperature.

Nutritional Information: Protein: 22g, Fat: 8g, Carbohydrates: 15g, Calories: 220

Beef and Pumpkin Omelette

Cooking Time: 20 minutes

Servings: 2

Ingredients:

- 1/2 cup cooked lean ground beef
- 1/4 cup canned pumpkin puree
- 4 eggs
- 1 tablespoon olive oil

Instructions:

1. In a bowl, mix together cooked ground beef and pumpkin puree until well combined.
2. In a separate bowl, whisk the eggs.
3. Heat olive oil in a skillet over medium heat.
4. Pour half of the whisked eggs into the skillet, spreading them evenly.
5. Cook until the edges start to set, then add half of the beef and pumpkin mixture to one side of the omelette.
6. Fold the other side of the omelette over the filling and cook for another 2-3 minutes, or until the eggs are fully cooked.
7. Repeat the process for the second omelette.
8. Let cool before serving to your dog.

Nutritional Information: Protein: 21g, Fat: 16g, Carbohydrates: 6g, Calories: 250

Tuna and Brown Rice Breakfast Bowl

Cooking Time: 15 minutes

Servings: 2

Ingredients:

- 1 can (5 oz) tuna in water, drained

- 1/2 cup cooked brown rice

- 1/4 cup cooked green beans, chopped

- 2 teaspoons olive oil

Instructions:

1. In a bowl, combine drained tuna, cooked brown rice, and chopped green beans.

2. Drizzle olive oil over the mixture and toss until well coated.

3. Divide the mixture into two bowls.

4. Serve at room temperature to your dog.

Nutritional Information: Protein: 22g, Fat: 8g, Carbohydrates: 20g, Calories: 280

Chicken and Carrot Frittata

Cooking Time: 25 minutes

Servings: 2

Ingredients:

- 1 cup cooked chicken, diced

- 1/2 cup grated carrots

- 4 eggs

- 1 tablespoon coconut oil

Instructions:

1. Preheat the oven to 350°F (175°C).

2. In a bowl, mix together diced chicken and grated carrots.

3. In a separate bowl, whisk the eggs.

4. Heat coconut oil in an oven-safe skillet over medium heat.

5. Pour the whisked eggs into the skillet, then add the chicken and carrot mixture on top.

6. Cook on the stovetop for 3-4 minutes, then transfer the skillet to the preheated oven.

7. Bake for 10-12 minutes, or until the eggs are fully set.

8. Let cool before serving to your dog.

Nutritional Information: Protein: 20g, Fat: 15g, Carbohydrates: 5g, Calories: 230

Pork and Apple Breakfast Patties

Cooking Time: 20 minutes

Servings: 4

Ingredients:

- 1 cup cooked lean ground pork

- 1 medium apple, grated

- 2 eggs

- 2 tablespoons coconut flour

Instructions:

1. In a bowl, combine cooked ground pork, grated apple, eggs, and coconut flour.

2. Mix well until all ingredients are evenly incorporated.

3. Divide the mixture into four portions and shape each portion into a patty.

4. Heat a non-stick skillet over medium heat and lightly grease with coconut oil.

5. Cook the patties for 5-7 minutes on each side, or until cooked through and golden brown.

6. Let cool before serving to your dog.

Nutritional Information: Protein: 15g, Fat: 10g, Carbohydrates: 5g, Calories: 180

Veggie and Egg Muffins

Cooking Time: 25 minutes

Servings: 6

Ingredients:

- 4 eggs

- 1/2 cup mixed vegetables (e.g., bell peppers, spinach, broccoli), finely chopped

- 1/4 cup shredded cheese (optional)

Instructions:

1. Preheat the oven to 350°F (175°C) and grease a muffin tin.

2. In a bowl, whisk the eggs until well beaten.

3. Stir in the chopped vegetables and shredded cheese, if using.

4. Pour the egg mixture into the prepared muffin tin, filling each cup about halfway.

5. Bake for 20-25 minutes, or until the muffins are set and lightly golden on top.

6. Let cool before serving to your dog.

Nutritional Information: Protein: 8g, Fat: 6g, Carbohydrates: 2g, Calories: 110

Lamb and Rice Porridge

Cooking Time: 30 minutes

Servings: 2

Ingredients:

- 1/2 cup cooked lamb, diced

- 1/4 cup cooked white rice

- 2 cups low-sodium chicken broth

- 1/4 cup chopped parsley (optional)

Instructions:

1. In a saucepan, combine diced lamb, cooked white rice, and chicken broth.

2. Bring the mixture to a boil over medium heat.

3. Reduce the heat to low and simmer for 20-25 minutes, stirring occasionally, until the porridge thickens.

4. Remove from heat and let cool slightly.

5. Stir in chopped parsley, if using.

6. Serve warm to your dog.

Nutritional Information: Protein: 18g, Fat: 10g, Carbohydrates: 15g, Calories: 220

Turkey and Zucchini Breakfast Bowl

Cooking Time: 20 minutes

Servings: 2

Ingredients:

- 1 cup cooked ground turkey

- 1 medium zucchini, grated

- 2 eggs

- 1 tablespoon olive oil

Instructions:

1. Heat olive oil in a skillet over medium heat.

2. Add grated zucchini to the skillet and cook until softened, about 3-4 minutes.

3. Add cooked ground turkey to the skillet and cook for an additional 2-3 minutes.

4. In a separate pan, fry the eggs to your desired doneness.

5. Divide the turkey and zucchini mixture onto two plates.

6. Top each serving with a fried egg.

7. Let cool before serving to your dog.

Nutritional Information: Protein: 20g, Fat: 12g, Carbohydrates: 5g, Calories: 200

CHAPER 4
Lunch and Dinner Options

Chicken and Rice Bowl

Cooking Time: 25 minutes

Servings: 2

Ingredients:

- 1 cup cooked chicken breast, diced

- 1/2 cup cooked brown rice

- 1/4 cup cooked green peas

- 1 tablespoon olive oil

Instructions:

1. In a skillet, heat olive oil over medium heat.

2. Add diced chicken breast to the skillet and cook until lightly browned, about 5 minutes.

3. Add cooked brown rice and green peas to the skillet, stirring until heated through, about 3-4 minutes.

4. Remove from heat and let cool before serving to your dog.

Nutritional Information: Protein: 20g, Fat: 10g, Carbohydrates: 15g, Calories: 220

Turkey and Vegetable Stir-Fry

Cooking Time: 20 minutes

Servings: 2

Ingredients:

- 1 cup cooked ground turkey

- 1/2 cup mixed vegetables (e.g., carrots, bell peppers, broccoli), sliced

- 1 tablespoon coconut oil

- 2 tablespoons low-sodium soy sauce (optional)

Instructions:

1. In a skillet, heat coconut oil over medium-high heat.

2. Add mixed vegetables to the skillet and stir-fry until tender-crisp, about 3-4 minutes.

3. Add cooked ground turkey to the skillet and cook for an additional 2-3 minutes.

4. If using, add low-sodium soy sauce to the skillet and toss to coat the ingredients evenly.

5. Remove from heat and let cool slightly before serving to your dog.

Nutritional Information: Protein: 18g, Fat: 12g, Carbohydrates: 8g, Calories: 230

Beef and Sweet Potato Stew

Cooking Time: 30 minutes

Servings: 2

Ingredients:

- 1 cup cooked lean beef, diced

- 1/2 cup cooked sweet potato, diced

- 1/4 cup cooked carrots, diced

- 1 cup low-sodium beef broth

Instructions:

1. In a saucepan, combine diced beef, sweet potato, carrots, and beef broth.

2. Bring the mixture to a boil over medium heat.

3. Reduce the heat to low and simmer for 15-20 minutes, stirring occasionally, until the stew thickens.

4. Remove from heat and let cool before serving to your dog.

Nutritional Information: Protein: 22g, Fat: 8g, Carbohydrates: 12g, Calories: 240

Salmon and Quinoa Salad

Cooking Time: 20 minutes

Servings: 2

Ingredients:

- 1 cup cooked salmon, flaked

- 1/2 cup cooked quinoa

- 1/4 cup cooked green beans, chopped

- 1 tablespoon olive oil

- 1 tablespoon lemon juice

Instructions:

1. In a bowl, combine flaked salmon, cooked quinoa, and chopped green beans.

2. Drizzle olive oil and lemon juice over the mixture and toss until well combined.

3. Divide the salad into two portions and serve to your dog.

Nutritional Information: Protein: 20g, Fat: 12g, Carbohydrates: 15g, Calories: 230

Tuna and Chickpea Salad

Cooking Time: 15 minutes

Servings: 2

Ingredients:

- 1 can (5 oz) tuna in water, drained

- 1/2 cup cooked chickpeas

- 1/4 cup diced cucumber

- 1 tablespoon plain Greek yogurt

Instructions:

1. In a bowl, combine drained tuna, cooked chickpeas, and diced cucumber.

2. Add plain Greek yogurt to the bowl and mix until well combined.

3. Divide the salad into two portions and serve to your dog.

Nutritional Information: Protein: 18g, Fat: 6g, Carbohydrates: 10g, Calories: 180

Turkey and Pumpkin Soup

Cooking Time: 25 minutes

Servings: 2

Ingredients:

- 1 cup cooked ground turkey

- 1/2 cup canned pumpkin puree

- 2 cups low-sodium chicken broth

- 1/4 cup cooked brown rice

Instructions:

1. In a saucepan, combine cooked ground turkey, pumpkin puree, and chicken broth.

2. Bring the mixture to a boil over medium heat.

3. Reduce the heat to low and simmer for 15-20 minutes, stirring occasionally.

4. Stir in cooked brown rice and continue to simmer for an additional 5 minutes.

5. Remove from heat and let cool slightly before serving to your dog.

Nutritional Information: Protein: 20g, Fat: 8g, Carbohydrates: 10g, Calories: 200

Chicken and Vegetable Skewers

Cooking Time: 20 minutes

Servings: 2

Ingredients:

- 1 cup cooked chicken breast, cubed

- 1/2 cup mixed vegetables (e.g., cherry tomatoes, zucchini, bell peppers), chopped

- Wooden skewers, soaked in water

Instructions:

1. Preheat the grill or grill pan over medium heat.

2. Thread alternating pieces of chicken and mixed vegetables onto the soaked wooden skewers.

3. Grill the skewers for 8-10 minutes, turning occasionally, until the chicken is cooked through and the vegetables are tender.

4. Remove from the grill and let cool slightly before serving to your dog.

Nutritional Information: Protein: 22g, Fat: 10g, Carbohydrates: 8g, Calories: 220

Beef and Barley Stew

Cooking Time: 30 minutes

Servings: 2

Ingredients:

- 1 cup cooked lean beef, diced

- 1/2 cup cooked barley

- 1/4 cup cooked carrots, diced

- 1 cup low-sodium beef broth

Instructions:

1. In a saucepan, combine diced beef, cooked barley, carrots, and beef broth.

2. Bring the mixture to a boil over medium heat.

3. Reduce the heat to low and simmer for 15-20 minutes, stirring occasionally, until the stew thickens.

4. Remove from heat and let cool before serving to your dog.

Nutritional Information: Protein: 20g, Fat: 8g, Carbohydrates: 15g, Calories: 220

Pork and Apple Casserole

Cooking Time: 35 minutes

Servings: 2

Ingredients:

- 1 cup cooked lean ground pork

- 1 medium apple, diced

- 1/2 cup cooked quinoa

- 1/4 cup low-sodium chicken broth

Instructions:

1. Preheat the oven to 350°F (175°C).

2. In a baking dish, combine cooked ground pork, diced apple, cooked quinoa, and chicken broth.

3. Mix until well combined.

4. Bake for 25-30 minutes, or until the casserole is heated through and the apples are tender.

5. Let cool before serving to your dog.

Nutritional Information: Protein: 18g, Fat: 10g, Carbohydrates: 15g, Calories: 220

Lamb and Spinach Salad

Cooking Time: 15 minutes

Servings: 2

Ingredients:

- 1 cup cooked lamb, diced

- 1 cup fresh spinach leaves

- 1/4 cup cherry tomatoes, halved

- 1 tablespoon olive oil

- 1 tablespoon balsamic vinegar

Instructions:

1. In a bowl, combine diced lamb, spinach leaves, and cherry tomatoes.

2. Drizzle olive oil and balsamic vinegar over the salad and toss until well coated.

3. Divide the salad into two portions and serve to your dog.

Nutritional Information: Protein: 22g, Fat: 12g, Carbohydrates: 8g, Calories: 230

CHAPTER 5
SOUPS

Chicken and Vegetable Soup

Cooking Time: 30 minutes

Servings: 4

Ingredients:

- 2 cups cooked chicken breast, shredded

- 1 cup mixed vegetables (carrots, peas, green beans), diced

- 4 cups low-sodium chicken broth

- 1/2 cup cooked brown rice

Instructions:

1. In a large pot, bring the chicken broth to a boil over medium heat.

2. Add the mixed vegetables and cooked chicken breast to the pot.

3. Simmer for 15 minutes until the vegetables are tender.

4. Stir in the cooked brown rice and simmer for an additional 5 minutes.

5. Let cool before serving to your dog.

Nutritional Information: Protein: 20g, Fat: 5g, Carbohydrates: 10g, Calories: 150

Beef and Barley Soup

Cooking Time: 45 minutes

Servings: 4

Ingredients:

- 2 cups cooked lean beef, diced

- 1/2 cup cooked barley

- 1 cup mixed vegetables (carrots, celery, green beans), diced

- 4 cups low-sodium beef broth

Instructions:

1. In a large pot, bring the beef broth to a boil over medium heat.

2. Add the diced beef, cooked barley, and mixed vegetables to the pot.

3. Reduce heat and simmer for 30 minutes until vegetables are tender.

4. Let cool slightly before serving to your dog.

Nutritional Information: Protein: 22g, Fat: 8g, Carbohydrates: 12g, Calories: 200

Turkey and Pumpkin Soup

Cooking Time: 25 minutes

Servings: 4

Ingredients:

- 2 cups cooked ground turkey

- 1 cup canned pumpkin puree

- 4 cups low-sodium chicken broth

- 1/4 cup cooked quinoa

Instructions:

1. In a large pot, bring the chicken broth to a boil over medium heat.

2. Add the cooked ground turkey and canned pumpkin puree to the pot.

3. Simmer for 15 minutes, stirring occasionally.

4. Stir in the cooked quinoa and simmer for an additional 5 minutes.

5. Let cool before serving to your dog.

Nutritional Information: Protein: 18g, Fat: 6g, Carbohydrates: 8g, Calories: 170

Salmon and Sweet Potato Chowder

Cooking Time: 35 minutes

Servings: 4

Ingredients:

- 2 cups cooked salmon, flaked

- 2 cups cooked sweet potato, mashed

- 4 cups low-sodium vegetable broth

- 1/2 cup cooked green peas

Instructions:

1. In a large pot, bring the vegetable broth to a boil over medium heat.

2. Add the mashed sweet potato to the pot and stir until well combined.

3. Add the flaked salmon and cooked green peas to the pot.

4. Simmer for 15 minutes, stirring occasionally.

5. Let cool slightly before serving to your dog.

Nutritional Information: Protein: 20g, Fat: 10g, Carbohydrates: 10g, Calories: 180

Chicken and Rice Congee

Cooking Time: 40 minutes

Servings: 4

Ingredients:

- 2 cups cooked chicken breast, shredded

- 1 cup cooked white rice

- 4 cups low-sodium chicken broth

- 1/4 cup chopped parsley (optional)

Instructions:

1. In a large pot, bring the chicken broth to a boil over medium heat.

2. Add the cooked chicken breast and white rice to the pot.

3. Simmer for 30 minutes, stirring occasionally.

4. Stir in chopped parsley, if using, and let cool before serving to your dog.

Nutritional Information: Protein: 20g, Fat: 5g, Carbohydrates: 10g, Calories: 150

Turkey and Vegetable Stew

Cooking Time: 35 minutes

Servings: 4

Ingredients:

- 2 cups cooked ground turkey

- 1 cup mixed vegetables (carrots, green beans, potatoes), diced

- 4 cups low-sodium chicken broth

- 1/4 cup cooked barley

Instructions:

1. In a large pot, bring the chicken broth to a boil over medium heat.

2. Add the mixed vegetables and cooked ground turkey to the pot.

3. Simmer for 20 minutes until the vegetables are tender.

4. Stir in the cooked barley and simmer for an additional 10 minutes.

5. Let cool before serving to your dog.

Nutritional Information: Protein: 18g, Fat: 6g, Carbohydrates: 8g, Calories: 170

Beef and Lentil Soup

Cooking Time: 40 minutes

Servings: 4

Ingredients:

- 2 cups cooked lean beef, diced
- 1 cup cooked lentils
- 1 cup mixed vegetables (carrots, onions, celery), diced
- 4 cups low-sodium beef broth

Instructions:

1. In a large pot, bring the beef broth to a boil over medium heat.
2. Add the diced beef, cooked lentils, and mixed vegetables to the pot.
3. Simmer for 30 minutes until the vegetables are tender.
4. Let cool slightly before serving to your dog.

Nutritional Information: Protein: 22g, Fat: 8g, Carbohydrates: 12g, Calories: 200

Chicken and Quinoa Soup

Cooking Time: 30 minutes

Servings: 4

Ingredients:

- 2 cups cooked chicken breast, shredded

- 1 cup cooked quinoa

- 1 cup mixed vegetables (carrots, peas, corn), diced

- 4 cups low-sodium chicken broth

Instructions:

1. In a large pot, bring the chicken broth to a boil over medium heat.

2. Add the shredded chicken breast, cooked quinoa, and mixed vegetables to the pot.

3. Simmer for 20 minutes until the vegetables are tender.

4. Let cool before serving to your dog.

Nutritional Information: Protein: 20g, Fat: 5g, Carbohydrates: 10g, Calories: 150

Salmon and Potato Chowder

Cooking Time: 35 minutes

Servings: 4

Ingredients:

- 2 cups cooked salmon, flaked

- 2 cups cooked potatoes, diced

- 4 cups low-sodium vegetable broth

- 1/2 cup cooked carrots, diced

Instructions:

1. In a large pot, bring the vegetable broth to a boil over medium heat.

2. Add the diced potatoes and cooked carrots to the pot.

3. Simmer for 20 minutes until the vegetables are tender.

4. Add the flaked salmon to the pot and simmer for an additional 10 minutes.

5. Let cool slightly before serving to your dog.

Nutritional Information: Protein: 20g, Fat: 10g, Carbohydrates: 10g, Calories: 180

Turkey and Bean Soup

Cooking Time: 40 minutes

Servings: 4

Ingredients:

- 2 cups cooked ground turkey

- 1 cup cooked kidney beans

- 1 cup mixed vegetables (carrots, celery, bell peppers), diced

- 4 cups low-sodium chicken broth

Instructions:

1. In a large pot, bring the chicken broth to a boil over medium heat.

2. Add the cooked ground turkey, cooked kidney beans, and mixed vegetables to the pot.

3. Simmer for 30 minutes until the vegetables are tender.

4. Let cool before serving to your dog.

Nutritional Information: Protein: 18g, Fat: 6g, Carbohydrates: 8g, Calories: 170

CHAPTER 6

Snacks and Desserts

Carrot and Apple Dog Treats

Cooking Time: 25 minutes

Servings: 12 treats

Ingredients:

- 1 cup grated carrots

- 1 cup grated apple

- 1/2 cup rolled oats

- 1/4 cup coconut flour

- 2 eggs

Instructions:

1. Preheat your oven to 350°F (175°C) and line a baking sheet with parchment paper.

2. In a large bowl, combine grated carrots, grated apple, rolled oats, coconut flour, and eggs. Mix until well combined.

3. Scoop tablespoon-sized portions of the mixture and roll into balls. Place them on the prepared baking sheet and flatten slightly with your fingers.

4. Bake in the preheated oven for 15-20 minutes until golden brown and firm.

5. Let cool completely before serving to your dog.

Nutritional Information: Protein: 2g, Fat: 1g, Carbohydrates: 5g, Calories: 35 per treat

Pumpkin and Peanut Butter Bites

Cooking Time: 20 minutes

Servings: 10 bites

Ingredients:

- 1 cup canned pumpkin puree

- 1/4 cup natural peanut butter (no added salt or sugar)

- 1/2 cup coconut flour

Instructions:

1. In a mixing bowl, combine pumpkin puree, peanut butter, and coconut flour. Mix until a dough forms.

2. Roll the dough into small balls and place them on a baking sheet lined with parchment paper.

3. Flatten each ball with a fork to create a cookie shape.

4. Bake in a preheated oven at 350°F (175°C) for 15 minutes until firm.

5. Allow to cool completely before serving to your dog.

Nutritional Information: Protein: 3g, Fat: 4g, Carbohydrates: 6g, Calories: 70 per bite

Blueberry and Banana Frozen Treats

Preparation Time: 10 minutes

Freezing Time: 4 hours

Servings: 6 treats

Ingredients:

- 1 ripe banana

- 1/2 cup fresh blueberries

- 1 cup plain Greek yogurt

Instructions:

1. Mash the ripe banana in a mixing bowl.

2. Add the fresh blueberries and plain Greek yogurt to the bowl. Mix until well combined.

3. Spoon the mixture into ice cube trays or silicone Molds.

4. Place in the freezer and freeze for at least 4 hours or until solid.

5. Pop the treats out of the Molds and store in a freezer-safe container.

6. Serve one treat to your dog as a refreshing snack.

Nutritional Information: Protein: 3g, Fat: 1g, Carbohydrates: 5g, Calories: 35 per treat

Chicken and Sweet Potato Jerky

Preparation Time: 10 minutes

Cooking Time: 3 hours

Servings: Variable

Ingredients:

- 2 boneless, skinless chicken breasts

- 1 medium sweet potato

Instructions:

1. Preheat your oven to 200°F (95°C) and line a baking sheet with parchment paper.

2. Slice the chicken breasts and sweet potato into thin strips.

3. Place the strips on the prepared baking sheet, ensuring they are not touching.

4. Bake in the preheated oven for 3 hours until the jerky is dried and crispy.

5. Let cool completely before serving to your dog.

6. Store leftovers in an airtight container in the refrigerator.

Nutritional Information: Protein: 15g (per 1 oz serving), Fat: 1g, Carbohydrates: 3g, Calories: 75 per 1 oz serving

Spinach and Cheese Dog Biscuits

Cooking Time: 30 minutes

Servings: 20 biscuits

Ingredients:

- 2 cups fresh spinach leaves

- 1/2 cup grated cheese (e.g., cheddar or mozzarella)

- 1 1/2 cups whole wheat flour

- 1/4 cup unsweetened applesauce

Instructions:

1. Preheat your oven to 350°F (175°C) and line a baking sheet with parchment paper.

2. In a food processor, blend the fresh spinach leaves until finely chopped.

3. In a mixing bowl, combine the chopped spinach, grated cheese, whole wheat flour, and unsweetened applesauce. Mix until a dough forms.

4. Roll out the dough on a floured surface to about 1/4 inch thickness.

5. Use cookie cutters to cut out shapes and place them on the prepared baking sheet.

6. Bake in the preheated oven for 20-25 minutes until golden brown.

7. Let cool completely before serving to your dog.

Nutritional Information: Protein: 2g, Fat: 1g, Carbohydrates: 5g, Calories: 35 per biscuit

Turkey and Cranberry Biscuits

Cooking Time: 25 minutes

Servings: 16 biscuits

Ingredients:

- 1 cup cooked ground turkey

- 1/4 cup dried cranberries (unsweetened)

- 1 1/2 cups oat flour

- 1 egg

Instructions:

1. Preheat your oven to 350°F (175°C) and line a baking sheet with parchment paper.

2. In a mixing bowl, combine the cooked ground turkey, dried cranberries, oat flour, and egg. Mix until well combined.

3. Roll out the dough on a floured surface to about 1/4 inch thickness.

4. Use cookie cutters to cut out shapes and place them on the prepared baking sheet.

5. Bake in the preheated oven for 20-25 minutes until golden brown.

6. Let cool completely before serving to your dog.

Nutritional Information: Protein: 3g, Fat: 2g, Carbohydrates: 5g, Calories: 45 per biscuit

Apple and Cinnamon Dog Cookies

Cooking Time: 30 minutes

Servings: 24 cookies

Ingredients:

- 1 cup unsweetened applesauce

- 1/2 cup rolled oats

- 1 1/2 cups oat flour

- 1 teaspoon ground cinnamon

Instructions:

1. Preheat your oven to 350°F (175°C) and line a baking sheet with parchment paper.

2. In a mixing bowl, combine the unsweetened applesauce, rolled oats, oat flour, and ground cinnamon. Mix until a dough forms.

3. Roll out the dough on a floured surface to about 1/4 inch thickness.

4. Use cookie cutters to cut out shapes and place them on the prepared baking sheet.

5. Bake in the preheated oven for 20-25 minutes until golden brown.

6. Let cool completely before serving to your dog.

Nutritional Information: Protein: 2g, Fat: 1g, Carbohydrates: 5g, Calories: 35 per cookie

Banana and Peanut Butter Popsicles

Preparation Time: 10 minutes

Freezing Time: 4 hours

Servings: 6 popsicles

Ingredients:

- 2 ripe bananas

- 1/4 cup natural peanut butter (no added salt or sugar)

- 1 cup plain Greek yogurt

Instructions:

1. In a blender, combine ripe bananas, peanut butter, and plain Greek yogurt. Blend until smooth.

2. Pour the mixture into popsicle Molds.

3. Insert popsicle sticks into each Mold.

4. Place in the freezer and freeze for at least 4 hours or until solid.

5. Run warm water over the molds to loosen the popsicles before serving to your dog.

Nutritional Information: Protein: 3g, Fat: 2g, Carbohydrates: 6g, Calories: 45 per popsicle

Frozen Watermelon Treats

Preparation Time: 10 minutes

Freezing Time: 4 hours

Servings: Variable

Ingredients:

- Fresh watermelon, cut into bite-sized pieces

Instructions:

1. Cut the watermelon into bite-sized pieces.

2. Place the pieces on a baking sheet lined with parchment paper.

3. Place in the freezer and freeze for at least 4 hours or until solid.

4. Serve a few frozen watermelon pieces to your dog as a refreshing snack.

Nutritional Information: Protein: 1g, Fat: 0g, Carbohydrates: 5g, Calories: 20 per 1 cup serving

Yogurt and Blueberry Bark

Preparation Time: 10 minutes

Freezing Time: 4 hours

Servings: Variable

Ingredients:

- Plain Greek yogurt

- Fresh blueberries

Instructions:

1. Line a baking sheet with parchment paper.

2. Spread a layer of plain Greek yogurt onto the parchment paper.

3. Scatter fresh blueberries evenly over the yogurt.

4. Place in the freezer and freeze for at least 4 hours or until solid.

5. Break the bark into pieces and serve to your dog as a cooling treat.

Nutritional Information: Protein: 3g, Fat: 2g, Carbohydrates: 6g, Calories: 45 per 1/4 cup serving

CHAPTER 7

Healthy Treats

Carrot and Apple Pup cakes

Cooking Time: 25 minutes

Servings: 12 pup cakes

Ingredients:

- 1 cup grated carrots

- 1 cup grated apple

- 1/2 cup coconut flour

- 1/4 cup unsweetened applesauce

- 2 eggs

- 1 teaspoon baking powder

Instructions:

1. Preheat your oven to 350°F (175°C) and line a muffin tin with paper liners.

2. In a mixing bowl, combine grated carrots, grated apple, coconut flour, unsweetened applesauce, eggs, and baking powder. Mix until well combined.

3. Divide the batter evenly among the muffin cups.

4. Bake in the preheated oven for 20-25 minutes until a toothpick inserted into the center comes out clean.

5. Let cool completely before serving to your dog.

Nutritional Information: Protein: 2g, Fat: 1g, Carbohydrates: 5g, Calories: 35 per pupcake

Banana and Peanut Butter Bites

Cooking Time: 20 minutes

Servings: 10 bites

Ingredients:

- 2 ripe bananas

- 1/4 cup natural peanut butter (no added salt or sugar)

- 1/2 cup rolled oats

Instructions:

1. Preheat your oven to 350°F (175°C) and line a baking sheet with parchment paper.

2. In a mixing bowl, mash the ripe bananas until smooth.

3. Add the natural peanut butter and rolled oats to the bowl. Mix until well combined.

4. Scoop tablespoon-sized portions of the mixture and roll into balls. Place them on the prepared baking sheet and flatten slightly with your fingers.

5. Bake in the preheated oven for 15-20 minutes until firm and golden brown.

6. Let cool completely before serving to your dog.

Nutritional Information: Protein: 3g, Fat: 4g, Carbohydrates: 6g, Calories: 70 per bite

Spinach and Cheese Cookies

Cooking Time: 25 minutes

Servings: 20 cookies

Ingredients:

- 2 cups fresh spinach leaves

- 1/2 cup grated cheese (e.g., cheddar or mozzarella)

- 1 1/2 cups oat flour

- 1/4 cup unsweetened applesauce

- 1 egg

Instructions:

1. Preheat your oven to 350°F (175°C) and line a baking sheet with parchment paper.

2. In a food processor, blend the fresh spinach leaves until finely chopped.

3. In a mixing bowl, combine the chopped spinach, grated cheese, oat flour, unsweetened applesauce, and egg. Mix until a dough forms.

4. Roll out the dough on a floured surface to about 1/4 inch thickness.

5. Use cookie cutters to cut out shapes and place them on the prepared baking sheet.

6. Bake in the preheated oven for 20-25 minutes until golden brown.

7. Let cool completely before serving to your dog.

Nutritional Information: Protein: 2g, Fat: 1g, Carbohydrates: 5g, Calories: 35 per cookie

Pumpkin and Oatmeal Balls

Cooking Time: 20 minutes

Servings: 12 balls

Ingredients:

- 1 cup canned pumpkin puree

- 1 cup rolled oats

- 1/4 cup unsweetened applesauce

- 1 teaspoon ground cinnamon

Instructions:

1. In a mixing bowl, combine canned pumpkin puree, rolled oats, unsweetened applesauce, and ground cinnamon. Mix until well combined.

2. Roll the mixture into tablespoon-sized balls and place them on a baking sheet lined with parchment paper.

3. Flatten each ball slightly with your fingers.

4. Bake in a preheated oven at 350°F (175°C) for 15-20 minutes until firm.

5. Let cool completely before serving to your dog.

Nutritional Information: Protein: 2g, Fat: 1g, Carbohydrates: 5g, Calories: 35 per ball

Chicken and Sweet Potato Muffins

Cooking Time: 30 minutes

Servings: 12 muffins

Ingredients:

- 1 cup cooked chicken breast, shredded

- 1 cup cooked sweet potato, mashed

- 1/2 cup coconut flour

- 1/4 cup unsweetened applesauce

- 2 eggs

Instructions:

1. Preheat your oven to 350°F (175°C) and line a muffin tin with paper liners.

2. In a mixing bowl, combine shredded chicken breast, mashed sweet potato, coconut flour, unsweetened applesauce, and eggs. Mix until well combined.

3. Divide the batter evenly among the muffin cups.

4. Bake in the preheated oven for 25-30 minutes until a toothpick inserted into the centre comes out clean.

5. Let cool completely before serving to your dog.

Nutritional Information: Protein: 3g, Fat: 2g, Carbohydrates: 6g, Calories: 45 per muffin

Turkey and Cranberry Biscuits

Cooking Time: 25 minutes

Servings: 16 biscuits

Ingredients:

- 1 cup cooked ground turkey

- 1/4 cup dried cranberries (unsweetened)

- 1 1/2 cups oat flour

- 1/4 cup unsweetened applesauce

- 1 egg

Instructions:

1. Preheat your oven to 350°F (175°C) and line a baking sheet with parchment paper.

2. In a mixing bowl, combine cooked ground turkey, dried cranberries, oat flour, unsweetened applesauce, and egg. Mix until well combined.

3. Roll out the dough on a floured surface to about 1/4 inch thickness.

4. Use cookie cutters to cut out shapes and place them on the prepared baking sheet.

5. Bake in the preheated oven for 20-25 minutes until golden brown.

6. Let cool completely before serving to your dog.

Nutritional Information: Protein: 3g, Fat: 2g, Carbohydrates: 5g, Calories: 45 per biscuit

Blueberry and Banana Muffins

Cooking Time: 25 minutes

Servings: 12 muffins

Ingredients:

- 2 ripe bananas, mashed

- 1/2 cup fresh blueberries

- 1 1/2 cups oat flour

- 1/4 cup unsweetened applesauce

- 2 eggs

Instructions:

1. Preheat your oven to 350°F (175°C) and line a muffin tin with paper liners.

2. In a mixing bowl, combine mashed bananas, fresh blueberries, oat flour, unsweetened applesauce, and eggs. Mix until well combined.

3. Divide the batter evenly among the muffin cups.

4. Bake in the preheated oven for 20-25 minutes until a toothpick inserted into the centre comes out clean.

5. Let cool completely before serving to your dog.

Nutritional Information: Protein: 2g, Fat: 1g, Carbohydrates: 5g, Calories: 35 per muffin

Salmon and Sweet Potato Cookies

Cooking Time: 30 minutes

Servings: 20 cookies

Ingredients:

- 1 cup cooked salmon, flaked

- 1 cup cooked sweet potato, mashed

- 1 1/2 cups oat flour

- 1/4 cup unsweetened applesauce

- 1 egg

Instructions:

1. Preheat your oven to 350°F (175°C) and line a baking sheet with parchment paper.

2. In a mixing bowl, combine flaked cooked salmon, mashed sweet potato, oat flour, unsweetened applesauce, and egg. Mix until well combined.

3. Roll out the dough on a floured surface to about 1/4 inch thickness.

4. Use cookie cutters to cut out shapes and place them on the prepared baking sheet.

5. Bake in the preheated oven for 20-25 minutes until golden brown.

6. Let cool completely before serving to your dog.

Nutritional Information: Protein: 3g, Fat: 2g, Carbohydrates: 5g, Calories: 45 per cookie

Turkey and Veggie Meatballs

Cooking Time: 25 minutes

Servings: 12 meatballs

Ingredients:

- 1 cup cooked ground turkey

- 1/2 cup mixed vegetables (carrots, peas, green beans), finely chopped

- 1/2 cup oat flour

- 1/4 cup unsweetened applesauce

- 1 egg

Instructions:

1. Preheat your oven to 350°F (175°C) and line a baking sheet with parchment paper.

2. In a mixing bowl, combine cooked ground turkey, finely chopped mixed vegetables, oat flour, unsweetened applesauce, and egg. Mix until well combined.

3. Roll the mixture into tablespoon-sized balls and place them on the prepared baking sheet.

4. Bake in the preheated oven for 20-25 minutes until cooked through.

5. Let cool completely before serving to your dog.

Nutritional Information: Protein: 3g, Fat: 2g, Carbohydrates: 5g, Calories: 45 per meatball

Chicken and Zucchini Biscuits

Cooking Time: 30 minutes

Servings: 16 biscuits

Ingredients:

- 1 cup cooked chicken breast, shredded

- 1/2 cup grated zucchini

- 1 1/2 cups oat flour

- 1/4 cup unsweetened applesauce

- 1 egg

Instructions:

1. Preheat your oven to 350°F (175°C) and line a baking sheet with parchment paper.

2. In a mixing bowl, combine shredded cooked chicken breast, grated zucchini, oat flour, unsweetened applesauce, and egg. Mix until well combined.

3. Roll out the dough on a floured surface to about 1/4 inch thickness.

4. Use cookie cutters to cut out shapes and place them on the prepared baking sheet.

5. Bake in the preheated oven for 20-25 minutes until golden brown.

6. Let cool completely before serving to your dog.

Nutritional Information: Protein: 3g, Fat: 2g, Carbohydrates: 5g, Calories: 45 per biscuit

CONCLUSION

As we come to the end of this culinary journey through the Dog Food Cookbook for Weight Management, I am filled with a profound sense of gratitude and hope. Gratitude for the opportunity to share my passion for canine nutrition with you, and hope for the positive impact it will have on the lives of your furry companions.

Throughout this cookbook, we have explored the transformative power of proper nutrition in supporting weight management, promoting vitality, and enhancing overall well-being in dogs. From wholesome breakfasts to satisfying dinners and everything in between, each recipe has been thoughtfully crafted to nourish your dog from the inside out.

But beyond the ingredients and measurements lies a deeper truth: the bond we share with our dogs is truly special. It is a bond built on love, trust, and unwavering loyalty—a bond that transcends words and defies explanation. And just as we strive to provide the best care for our canine companions, they, in turn, enrich our lives in ways we could never imagine.

As you embark on your journey with this cookbook, I encourage you to embrace the opportunity to connect with your dog on a deeper level. Take the time to savor each moment spent preparing meals together, sharing nutritious and delicious dishes, and basking in the joy of a happy, healthy dog by your side.

I invite you to share your experiences, thoughts, and feedback with me. Your honest reviews and valuable insights will not only help me improve future editions of this cookbook but also contribute to our collective understanding of canine nutrition and well-being.

Together, let us continue to nourish our dogs, nurture our bond, and celebrate the joy of sharing our lives with these remarkable creatures.

Thank you for joining me on this journey. Here's to many more happy, healthy years with our beloved canine companions.

BONUS 1

Weight Loss Exercise Tips for Dogs

Incorporating regular exercise into your dog's routine is essential for maintaining their overall health and well-being, especially when it comes to managing their weight. Just like humans, dogs' benefit from physical activity to burn calories, build muscle, improve cardiovascular health, and boost their metabolism. In this chapter, we will explore the importance of exercise in canine weight loss, discuss different types of exercises suitable for dogs, provide guidelines for developing an exercise routine, and offer tips for safely and effectively exercising your dog to support their weight loss journey.

Importance of Exercise in Canine Weight Loss:

Regular exercise plays a crucial role in helping dogs achieve and maintain a healthy weight. Here are some key reasons why exercise is important for canine weight loss:

1. **Burns Calories:** Physical activity helps dogs burn excess calories, leading to weight loss when combined with a balanced diet.

2. **Increases Metabolism:** Exercise boosts a dog's metabolism, allowing them to burn calories more efficiently even when at rest.

3. **Builds Muscle:** Engaging in strength-building exercises helps dogs develop lean muscle mass, which can contribute to a higher metabolic rate and improved body composition.

4. **Improves Cardiovascular Health:** Aerobic exercises such as walking, running, and swimming strengthen the heart and lungs, promoting cardiovascular health in dogs.

5. **Enhances Mental Well-being:** Exercise provides mental stimulation and enrichment for dogs, reducing boredom, stress, and anxiety, which can contribute to overeating and weight gain.

Types of Exercises for Dogs:

There are various types of exercises that dogs can engage in to support weight loss and overall fitness. Some popular options include:

1. **Walking:** Regular brisk walks are an excellent form of low-impact exercise for dogs of all ages and fitness levels. Aim for at least 30 minutes of walking per day, gradually increasing the duration and intensity as your dog's fitness improves.

2. **Running/Jogging:** For more active dogs, running or jogging can provide a higher-intensity workout. Start with short intervals of running interspersed with walking and gradually increase the running time as your dog builds endurance.

3. **Swimming:** Swimming is a low-impact exercise that is gentle on the joints and muscles, making it ideal for dogs with joint issues or arthritis. Swimming engages multiple muscle groups and provides an excellent cardiovascular workout.

4. **Fetch/Frisbee:** Playing fetch or frisbee engages dogs both mentally and physically, providing aerobic exercise while also stimulating their natural chasing instincts. Use a ball or frisbee to encourage your dog to run, jump, and retrieve the toy.

5. **Agility Training:** Agility courses and obstacles offer a fun and challenging workout for dogs, incorporating activities such as jumping, weaving, climbing, and crawling. Agility training not only provides physical exercise but also mental stimulation and improves coordination and flexibility.

6. **Hiking:** Exploring nature trails and hiking paths allows dogs to experience new sights, smells, and terrain while getting a good workout. Hiking provides both aerobic and muscle-strengthening benefits, making it an excellent option for dogs with high energy levels.

Developing an Exercise Routine:

When developing an exercise routine for your dog, consider the following guidelines:

1. **Consult with Your Veterinarian:** Before starting any exercise program, consult with your veterinarian to ensure that your dog is healthy enough for physical activity and to discuss any specific considerations or restrictions based on their age, breed, health status, and existing medical conditions.

2. **Start Slowly:** Begin with low-intensity exercises and gradually increase the duration, frequency, and intensity as your dog's fitness level improves. Avoid overexertion, especially for older dogs or those with pre-existing health issues.

3. **Provide Variety:** Incorporate a mix of different types of exercises to keep your dog engaged and prevent boredom. Rotate between walking, running, swimming, and other activities to provide a well-rounded workout.

4. **Be Consistent:** Establish a regular exercise routine and stick to it. Aim for daily exercise sessions of at least 30 minutes to an hour, depending on your dog's needs and energy level.

5. **Monitor Progress:** Keep track of your dog's progress by monitoring their weight, body condition, endurance, and overall fitness level. Adjust the exercise routine as needed based on their response and results.

6. **Listen to Your Dog:** Pay attention to your dog's cues and signals during exercise. Watch for signs of fatigue, discomfort, or overexertion, and adjust the intensity or duration accordingly. Always prioritize your dog's safety and well-being.

Tips for Safe and Effective Exercise:

To ensure a safe and effective exercise experience for your dog, consider the following tips:

1. **Warm-Up and Cool Down:** Begin each exercise session with a gentle warm-up, such as a few minutes of walking, to prepare your dog's muscles and joints for activity. Similarly, end the session with a gradual cool-down to help prevent stiffness and reduce the risk of injury.

2. **Stay Hydrated:** Provide plenty of fresh water before, during, and after exercise to keep your dog hydrated, especially in warm weather or during intense workouts. Watch for signs of dehydration, such as excessive panting or lethargy, and take breaks as needed.

3. **Protect Their Paws:** Check your dog's paw pads regularly for any cuts, abrasions, or signs of irritation, especially if exercising on rough surfaces or hot pavement. Consider using paw balms or booties to provide additional protection and prevent injuries.

4. **Avoid Extreme Weather:** Exercise caution when exercising your dog in extreme weather conditions, such as high heat, humidity, or cold

temperatures. Limit outdoor activities during peak sun hours and provide shade and access to water to prevent heatstroke or hypothermia.

5. **Use Proper Equipment:** Invest in quality gear such as a sturdy leash, harness, or life jacket (for swimming) to ensure your dog's safety during exercise. Choose equipment that fits properly and allows for freedom of movement without causing discomfort or restriction.

6. **Supervise Off-Leash Activities:** If allowing your dog off-leash, ensure they are in a safe and enclosed area free from hazards such as traffic, wildlife, or steep terrain. Maintain supervision at all times to prevent accidents or encounters with other animals.

BONUS 2
30 Day Meal plan

Day	Breakfast	Lunch	Dinner	Snacks
1	Turkey & Sweet Potato Hash	Chicken & Vegetable Stir-Fry	Salmon & Sweet Potato Casserole	Carrot & Apple Pup cakes
2	Banana & Peanut Butter Pancakes	Turkey & Veggie Meatballs	Chicken & Zucchini Biscuits	Blueberry & Banana Muffins
3	Spinach & Cheese Omelets	Turkey & Cranberry Biscuits	Pumpkin & Oatmeal Balls	Frozen Watermelon Treats
4	Apple & Cinnamon Oatmeal	Chicken & Sweet Potato Muffins	Turkey & Veggie Meatballs	Yogurt & Blueberry Bark
5	Turkey & Cranberry Biscuits	Salmon & Sweet Potato Casserole	Spinach & Cheese Cookies	Frozen Watermelon Treats
6	Banana & Peanut Butter Bites	Turkey & Veggie Meatballs	Chicken & Zucchini Biscuits	Yogurt & Blueberry Bark
7	Blueberry & Banana Smoothie	Chicken & Vegetable Stir-Fry	Salmon & Sweet Potato Casserole	Carrot & Apple Pup cakes

8	Turkey & Sweet Potato Hash	Chicken & Sweet Potato Muffins	Pumpkin & Oatmeal Balls	Blueberry & Banana Muffins
9	Spinach & Cheese Omelets	Turkey & Cranberry Biscuits	Turkey & Veggie Meatballs	Frozen Watermelon Treats
10	Apple & Cinnamon Oatmeal	Banana & Peanut Butter Pancakes	Chicken & Zucchini Biscuits	Yogurt & Blueberry Bark
11	Turkey & Cranberry Biscuits	Chicken & Vegetable Stir-Fry	Salmon & Sweet Potato Casserole	Carrot & Apple Pup cakes
12	Banana & Peanut Butter Bites	Turkey & Veggie Meatballs	Spinach & Cheese Cookies	Frozen Watermelon Treats
13	Blueberry & Banana Smoothie	Chicken & Sweet Potato Muffins	Turkey & Veggie Meatballs	Yogurt & Blueberry Bark
14	Turkey & Sweet Potato Hash	Salmon & Sweet Potato Casserole	Pumpkin & Oatmeal Balls	Blueberry & Banana Muffins
15	Spinach & Cheese Omelets	Turkey & Cranberry Biscuits	Chicken & Zucchini Biscuits	Frozen Watermelon Treats
16	Apple & Cinnamon Oatmeal	Banana & Peanut Butter Pancakes	Turkey & Veggie Meatballs	Yogurt & Blueberry Bark

17	Turkey & Cranberry Biscuits	Chicken & Vegetable Stir-Fry	Salmon & Sweet Potato Casserole	Carrot & Apple Pupcakes
18	Banana & Peanut Butter Bites	Turkey & Veggie Meatballs	Spinach & Cheese Cookies	Frozen Watermelon Treats
19	Blueberry & Banana Smoothie	Chicken & Sweet Potato Muffins	Chicken & Zucchini Biscuits	Yogurt & Blueberry Bark
20	Turkey & Sweet Potato Hash	Salmon & Sweet Potato Casserole	Pumpkin & Oatmeal Balls	Blueberry & Banana Muffins
21	Spinach & Cheese Omelets	Turkey & Cranberry Biscuits	Turkey & Veggie Meatballs	Frozen Watermelon Treats
22	Apple & Cinnamon Oatmeal	Banana & Peanut Butter Pancakes	Chicken & Zucchini Biscuits	Yogurt & Blueberry Bark
23	Turkey & Cranberry Biscuits	Chicken & Vegetable Stir-Fry	Salmon & Sweet Potato Casserole	Carrot & Apple Pupcakes
24	Banana & Peanut Butter Bites	Turkey & Veggie Meatballs	Spinach & Cheese Cookies	Frozen Watermelon Treats
25	Blueberry & Banana Smoothie	Chicken & Sweet Potato Muffins	Turkey & Veggie Meatballs	Yogurt & Blueberry Bark

26	Turkey & Sweet Potato Hash	Salmon & Sweet Potato Casserole	Pumpkin & Oatmeal Balls	Blueberry & Banana Muffins
27	Spinach & Cheese Omelets	Turkey & Cranberry Biscuits	Chicken & Zucchini Biscuits	Frozen Watermelon Treats
28	Apple & Cinnamon Oatmeal	Banana & Peanut Butter Pancakes	Turkey & Veggie Meatballs	Yogurt & Blueberry Bark
29	Turkey & Cranberry Biscuits	Chicken & Vegetable Stir-Fry	Salmon & Sweet Potato Casserole	Carrot & Apple Pupcakes
30	Banana & Peanut Butter Bites	Turkey & Veggie Meatballs	Spinach & Cheese Cookies	Frozen Watermelon Treats

MEAL PLANNER JOURNAL

Meal Planner

Week of:

Monday	**Tuesday**	**Wednesday**
BREAKFAST	BREAKFAST	BREAKFAST
LUNCH	LUNCH	LUNCH
DINNER	DINNER	DINNER
SNACK	SNACK	SNACK
Thursday	**Friday**	**Saturday**
BREAKFAST	BREAKFAST	BREAKFAST
LUNCH	LUNCH	LUNCH
DINNER	DINNER	DINNER
SNACK	SNACK	SNACK
Sunday	NOTES:	
BREAKFAST		
LUNCH		
DINNER		
SNACK		

Meal Planner

Week of:

<table>
<tr><td>

Monday

BREAKFAST

LUNCH

DINNER

SNACK

</td><td>

Tuesday

BREAKFAST

LUNCH

DINNER

SNACK

</td><td>

Wednesday

BREAKFAST

LUNCH

DINNER

SNACK

</td></tr>
<tr><td>

Thursday

BREAKFAST

LUNCH

DINNER

SNACK

</td><td>

Friday

BREAKFAST

LUNCH

DINNER

SNACK

</td><td>

Saturday

BREAKFAST

LUNCH

DINNER

SNACK

</td></tr>
<tr><td>

Sunday

BREAKFAST

LUNCH

DINNER

SNACK

</td><td colspan="2">

NOTES:

</td></tr>
</table>

Meal Planner

Week of:

Monday	**Tuesday**	**Wednesday**
BREAKFAST	BREAKFAST	BREAKFAST
LUNCH	LUNCH	LUNCH
DINNER	DINNER	DINNER
SNACK	SNACK	SNACK
Thursday	**Friday**	**Saturday**
BREAKFAST	BREAKFAST	BREAKFAST
LUNCH	LUNCH	LUNCH
DINNER	DINNER	DINNER
SNACK	SNACK	SNACK

Sunday	NOTES:
BREAKFAST	
LUNCH	
DINNER	
SNACK	

Meal Planner

Week of:

Monday

BREAKFAST

LUNCH

DINNER

SNACK

Tuesday

BREAKFAST

LUNCH

DINNER

SNACK

Wednesday

BREAKFAST

LUNCH

DINNER

SNACK

Thursday

BREAKFAST

LUNCH

DINNER

SNACK

Friday

BREAKFAST

LUNCH

DINNER

SNACK

Saturday

BREAKFAST

LUNCH

DINNER

SNACK

Sunday

BREAKFAST

LUNCH

DINNER

SNACK

NOTES:

Meal Planner

Week of:

Monday	Tuesday	Wednesday
BREAKFAST	BREAKFAST	BREAKFAST
LUNCH	LUNCH	LUNCH
DINNER	DINNER	DINNER
SNACK	SNACK	SNACK

Thursday	Friday	Saturday
BREAKFAST	BREAKFAST	BREAKFAST
LUNCH	LUNCH	LUNCH
DINNER	DINNER	DINNER
SNACK	SNACK	SNACK

Sunday	NOTES:
BREAKFAST	
LUNCH	
DINNER	
SNACK	

Meal Planner

Week of:

	Monday		Tuesday		Wednesday

Monday

BREAKFAST

LUNCH

DINNER

SNACK

Tuesday

BREAKFAST

LUNCH

DINNER

SNACK

Wednesday

BREAKFAST

LUNCH

DINNER

SNACK

Thursday

BREAKFAST

LUNCH

DINNER

SNACK

Friday

BREAKFAST

LUNCH

DINNER

SNACK

Saturday

BREAKFAST

LUNCH

DINNER

SNACK

Sunday

BREAKFAST

LUNCH

DINNER

SNACK

NOTES:

Meal Planner

Week of:

Monday		Tuesday		Wednesday
BREAKFAST		BREAKFAST		BREAKFAST
LUNCH		LUNCH		LUNCH
DINNER		DINNER		DINNER
SNACK		SNACK		SNACK

Thursday		Friday		Saturday
BREAKFAST		BREAKFAST		BREAKFAST
LUNCH		LUNCH		LUNCH
DINNER		DINNER		DINNER
SNACK		SNACK		SNACK

Sunday	NOTES:
BREAKFAST	
LUNCH	
DINNER	
SNACK	

Meal Planner

Week of:

Monday	**Tuesday**	**Wednesday**
BREAKFAST	BREAKFAST	BREAKFAST
LUNCH	LUNCH	LUNCH
DINNER	DINNER	DINNER
SNACK	SNACK	SNACK
Thursday	**Friday**	**Saturday**
BREAKFAST	BREAKFAST	BREAKFAST
LUNCH	LUNCH	LUNCH
DINNER	DINNER	DINNER
SNACK	SNACK	SNACK

Sunday	NOTES:
BREAKFAST	
LUNCH	
DINNER	
SNACK	

Meal Planner

Week of:

Monday
BREAKFAST
LUNCH
DINNER
SNACK

Tuesday
BREAKFAST
LUNCH
DINNER
SNACK

Wednesday
BREAKFAST
LUNCH
DINNER
SNACK

Thursday
BREAKFAST
LUNCH
DINNER
SNACK

Friday
BREAKFAST
LUNCH
DINNER
SNACK

Saturday
BREAKFAST
LUNCH
DINNER
SNACK

Sunday
BREAKFAST
LUNCH
DINNER
SNACK

NOTES:

Meal Planner

Week of:

Monday	Tuesday	Wednesday
BREAKFAST	BREAKFAST	BREAKFAST
LUNCH	LUNCH	LUNCH
DINNER	DINNER	DINNER
SNACK	SNACK	SNACK

Thursday	Friday	Saturday
BREAKFAST	BREAKFAST	BREAKFAST
LUNCH	LUNCH	LUNCH
DINNER	DINNER	DINNER
SNACK	SNACK	SNACK

Sunday	NOTES:
BREAKFAST	
LUNCH	
DINNER	
SNACK	

Meal Planner

Month of:

Sun	Mon	Tues	Wed	Thurs	Fri	Sai